CHICANO LIBERATION
and
SOCIALISM

Miguel Pendás

PATHFINDER
NEW YORK   LONDON   MONTREAL   SYDNEY

Copyright © 1976 by Pathfinder Press
All rights reserved

ISBN 978-0-87348-384-1
Library of Congress Control Number 2010928489
Manufactured in Canada

COVER PHOTO: Los Angeles, January 1971. March of 10,000 protests cop murder of Chicano youth Gustav Montag. (John Gray/Militant)

First edition, 1976
Twelfth printing, 2025

PATHFINDER
pathfinderpress.com
Email: pathfinder@pathfinderpress.com

Chicano liberation and socialism

MIGUEL PENDÁS

IN APRIL 1975, a delegation of Raza Unida party activists from throughout the country made a visit to Cuba at the invitation of the Cuban government. The head of the delegation, José Ángel Gutiérrez, held a news conference upon their return. This is how the *Chicano Times* summarized his description of Cuba: "A place where there is no hunger or poverty, a place where unemployment does not exist, a place where all the people get whatever medical attention that they need, a place where every family has a home and all the residents receive as much education that they want as long as they have a desire to learn."

Gutiérrez declared that the problems of poverty and racism suffered by Chicanos in Texas were similar to those that the Cuban people have begun to overcome by taking socialist measures.

One of the reporters then said to Gutiérrez, "You are going to be asked sometime that if you like socialism so much why don't you and all the other Mexicans go to Cuba."

Gutiérrez replied, "Because we are going to make a Cuba over here."

The response of the Raza Unida delegation to what they saw in Cuba is only one reflection of the growing interest among Chicanos in the revolutionary struggles of oppressed peoples in other parts of the world, as well as in the prospects for revolutionary change in this country.

Chicanos have not fared very well—to put it mildly—under the existing system of capitalism. Unemployment is estimated at up to 45 percent in barrios such as East Los Angeles. Prices continue to climb. The government is now trying to scrap many of the gains that Chicanos have made in the past few years. Affirmative action plans, bilingual and bicultural education programs, and Chicano studies are either not being implemented or are being cut back to the point where their very existence is threatened.

In addition, the war in Vietnam, the Pentagon papers, and the revelations about Watergate, the FBI, and the CIA have opened the eyes of millions of people, including Chicanos, to some of the truth about the real methods of capitalist rule. John F. Kennedy, whom many Chicanos thought to be an honest politician, is shown to be like all the rest. Kennedy—like Johnson and Nixon—plotted mass extermination programs in Vietnam, spying and disruption against the Black civil rights movement, and assassinations of African and Latin American leaders who did not fit in with Washington's plans.

Is socialism relevant to Chicanos?
Most Chicano activists do not begin as socialists. They begin by working to eliminate some of the particular injustices of this system rather than to replace it with a new system. But in the process of trying to do this, people come to realize that the injustices are a vital part of the system.

Many are led to the correct conclusion that there is something wrong with capitalism itself. Growing numbers are asking themselves whether socialism could work and, most of all, "Is it relevant to me as a Chicano?"

One question that is raised is, "Won't racism exist in any kind of society, capitalist or socialist?" This question arises because racism is so pervasive in this country that it is hard to envision a nonracist America.

Marxists think racism can be eliminated because its roots are not in "human nature" but in a particular social system: Capitalism. History and anthropology show that slavery, conquest, and oppression of one people by another arose with the division of society into classes, with a privileged few owning the wealth. This reached its peak under capitalism.

Racism originated with the African slave trade that developed in the early stages of capitalism. The theories of inferiority of peoples of color were developed and promoted to justify this enslavement of Africans and later the imperialist conquest of Africa, Asia, and Latin America.

While slavery was abolished in the U.S. in 1865, the capitalist rulers soon began to foster racism for another reason: To divide and disorient all the exploited and oppressed.

After 200 years, it is clearer than ever that American capitalism is totally dependent on the superexploitation of racial minorities. The average Chicano family earns only about 70 percent of what the average Anglo family earns. The same is true for Blacks. Where does the remaining 30 percent go? The capitalists pocket this money that they don't have to pay out in wages because of racism. Furthermore, the capitalists' overall economic and political power is strengthened indirectly by the divisive role of racism among the working people.

The capitalist system is hooked on racism. It will never give up its fix—the superprofits that come from being able to condemn Blacks, Chicanos, Puerto Ricans, and other oppressed minorities to the worst jobs, the worst schools, and the worst housing.

A society that abolishes exploitation for private profit, on the other hand, would have no such inherent drive to foster racism. Even before a socialist system is built, the struggle to achieve it will deal heavy blows to racist attitudes. The abolition of capitalism can only come about through a mass mobilization of all working people that must encompass a forthright struggle against racism.

One of the difficulties Chicanos encounter when assessing the relevance of socialism is that some people who claim to be Marxists have declared their hostility to Chicano nationalism, the concept of Chicano pride and unity that has infused the development of the Chicano movement of today. They say there is a contradiction between Chicano nationalism and the socialist concepts of class struggle and internationalism.

The most vocal exponents of antinationalism today are the Maoist groups. These include the October League, the Revolutionary Communist party (formerly Revolutionary Union), and the supporters of the *Guardian* newspaper. There are other smaller, local Maoist groupings, including some Chicano Maoist groups.

While there are shades of difference in their views, basically they share the position that struggles of Chicanos as a people are a diversion or, at best, a secondary aspect of "the class struggle," by which they mean struggles between workers and capitalists.

The Communist party has also declared its hostility to Chicano nationalism, calling it racism in reverse. In August 1975, for example, the CP had a meeting to honor the head of their Chicano Liberation Commission, Lorenzo Torres. The highest praise the CP leaders had for him was, "At a time when nationalism and the call for nationhood was high, Lorenzo fought for a working-class approach"—in other words, against nationalism.

Upon hearing statements like these in the name of Marxism and socialism, it is not surprising that some Chicano militants give up on the whole idea of socialism.

At the same time, there are some Chicano activists attracted to the idea of socialism who become confused in another way. Even though they themselves have been radicalized and have come to grasp the need for socialism through their experience in the nationalist Chicano movement, they think they must reject nationalism in order to embrace socialism.

Both are making a mistake.

Marxism begins from the premise that human history is basically the history of struggle between classes. But this general truth does not at all imply that nationalist struggles of oppressed peoples are a diversion from the class struggle. In fact, such national liberation struggles are a powerful component of the class struggle and are complementary to the development of revolutionary internationalism.

Related to the notion that "class struggle" in the abstract is more revolutionary than struggle by an oppressed people is the equally erroneous concept that "workers' issues" are revolutionary while Chicano issues are low level or irrelevant.

Sometimes you will see antinationalists at a Chicano demonstration trying to "educate" the participants on this question. While slogans such as "Viva la raza," "Chicano Power," or "La raza unida jamás será vencida" (Chicanos united will never be defeated) are being chanted, they remain silent. Then, when there is a pause, they start up with what they consider more "revolutionary" slogans, such as "*Obreros* unidos jamás serán vencidos" (Workers united will never be defeated).

Another example occurred at a 1974 demonstration in Los Angeles protesting the colonial status of Puerto Rico. The main slogan was "Independence for Puerto Rico," a nationalist demand that Marxists fully support. However, the Maoists of the Revolutionary Union (now Revolutionary Communist party) did not like this demand. They organized their followers into a contingent and sang the "International." Needless to say, very few people outside their circle knew what they were singing or why.

This is not a Marxist approach. So-called workers' issues—such as demands for higher wages and better conditions on the job—are an important part of the class struggle. But wage exploitation is not the only kind of oppression that exists under capitalism. There is also national oppression and the oppression of women, as well as special forms of oppression against youth, old people, gay people, and others. These are all forms of capitalist oppression, and most of their weight falls on the working class.

What is the class struggle?

The Marxist concept of the class struggle is not simply, or most fundamentally, the struggle by workers for higher wages or other trade-union demands. It is the struggle of the working class and its allies on all fronts, including on social and political issues, against the capitalist rulers.

In the case of the Chicano people, the interconnection of class and national oppression is very clear. The forms of oppression suffered by Chicanos as workers and as Chicanos are inseparable. Therefore, a socialist program must address itself to both.

In looking back over the experiences of the Chicano people in the past decade, we see that struggles directed to the needs of Chicanos as a people, far from retarding the class struggle or being irrelevant to it, have deepened and advanced it.

One of the best examples of this is the United Farm Workers movement. One reason that the UFW has been more successful than any other agricultural union is that it arose as an expression of the Chicano movement. There was no labor upsurge when the UFW began organizing. In fact, the trade-union movement was fairly quiet. It was Chicanos who were on the move, fighting against racist discrimination. And it was the Chicano community that saw the struggle of the farm workers as its own struggle and formed the backbone of the movement.

Chicano farm workers were attracted to this movement—*la causa*—because it spoke to their needs. It offered a means to combat their oppression both as workers and as Chicanos.

At the same time, the United Farm Workers have probably done more than any other union to revive the traditions of militant unionism in this country. After winning support in the barrios, the UFW boycott won support among both Blacks and Anglos in the cities.

The farm workers support movement grew strong enough

to force even the AFL-CIO bureaucrats to give it token support. The struggle has become so well known that support for the UFW is an important issue in many unions, including those located in the big cities of the North and East. It was also a key issue at the 1974 founding conference of the Coalition of Labor Union Women.

When the Teamsters union bureaucracy launched its raids on the UFW in 1973, the AFL-CIO bureaucracy felt compelled to back up the *campesinos* with more than a million dollars (something it should have done long ago). Rarely have the Teamster bureaucrats—for whom sweetheart deals and union raiding are a way of life—encountered such opposition. Chicanos are leading a struggle of workers for militant and democratic unionism against an entrenched bureaucracy that controls the biggest union in the country.

But this is not the only struggle of Chicanos as a people that has had an impact. In Los Angeles, Chicanos were in the forefront of the movement to get the United States out of Vietnam. In 1970, 30,000 Chicanos protested the war in the National Chicano Moratorium, held in East Los Angeles. This was the biggest antiwar demonstration ever held in that city up to that time. This internationalist action in solidarity with the people of Vietnam was a product of Chicano nationalism. Chicanos were saying: We refuse to die in a war of our oppressors!

The struggles against racism in the schools, for bilingual and bicultural education, for more Chicano teachers, for better jobs and higher wages for Chicanos, for job training, for more college admissions, for better housing, for Chicano studies—all of these struggles are part of the class struggle of the exploited against the exploiters. They are directed against the racist injustices that are part of the political, economic, and social fabric of capitalist society and that function to bolster the power and wealth of the ruling rich.

The Maoists and other sectarians claim that Chicano nationalist demands divide the working class and stand in the way of unity between Chicano and Anglo workers in struggle against their common oppressor. What they are really saying is that Chicanos should lay aside their legitimate grievances in order not to offend racist white workers. But this is hardly a way to achieve unity.

It is not the aspirations and struggles of Chicanos as a people that divide the working class; working people are divided by racist discrimination. The capitalist rulers foster and maintain racism by granting privileges to whites at the expense of Blacks, Puerto Ricans, Chicanos, and other oppressed minorities. As long as whites accept this situation, the basis for unity will be narrow indeed.

By fighting against racism and for equality, Chicanos and other oppressed peoples are pointing the way to the basis for real unity.

It *is* possible to win white working people to support the demands of the oppressed minorities. It will happen in two ways. First, it will happen as whites see that Chicanos and others will no longer tolerate racism and prejudice. For example, the Black civil rights struggles and ghetto rebellions of the 1960s had a major impact in increasing sensitivity and opposition to racism among whites.

White working people can also overcome their racist attitudes in action when they see in the course of their own struggles that in order to defeat the common enemy—the capitalist class—a common struggle is necessary. This is illustrated in the support that the UFW has received from unions that are not primarily Chicano. Non-Chicano workers are able to see that the attack on the farm workers is an attack on the right of all workers to form unions.

Is Chicano nationalism 'bourgeois'?
One of the contentions of those who oppose Chicano nationalism in the name of Marxism is that nationalism is a bourgeois ideology and leads to abandoning the class struggle. Nationalist movements, they claim, are led by bourgeois or petty-bourgeois (that is, capitalist or middle-class) forces, rather than by the working people of the oppressed nationalities.

Some Maoists think they have found a middle ground. They say they support only *some* struggles against national oppression—those waged by Chicano workers!

The main task of socialists, they argue, is to draw the class line between the Chicano workers and allegedly bourgeois and petty-bourgeois Chicanos. So, for example, they might support a strike by Chicano unionists, but not a struggle for more Chicanos on campus. If more Chicanos are able to go to college, you see, they'll just become "bourgeois."

By creating a phantom Chicano capitalist class, these Maoists relieve themselves of the duty to struggle against the real capitalist class and its ideology, which holds that the universities and the professions are for whites only.

Hypocritically, the Communist party also slanders the Chicano nationalist movement by saying that it leads to a multiclass alliance. However, while opposing the nationalist movement as divisive, bourgeois, and even reactionary, the CP urges Chicanos to support "progressive" capitalist politicians of the Democratic party as a way to gain their liberation.

The two-party trap

The Democrats are running more Chicanos for office now, but the number is still so small that it barely approaches tokenism. But is pushing for more Chicano Democrats in office going to help the mass of Chicanos? Chicanos can learn from the experience of the Black community in this regard.

Ten years ago there were hardly any Black elected officials. But under pressure of the Black struggle, the Democratic party began to run more and more Blacks for office. Black elected officials now number 3,500. Some hold high state and national office. Others are mayors of major cities, including Los Angeles, Newark, Atlanta, and Detroit. There are Black members of Congress. But despite all this the oppression and exploitation of Blacks is unchanged.

There is no reason to think it will be different for Chicanos.

It wasn't long after taking office in 1974 that Gov. Raul Castro of Arizona sent state troopers to attack a lemonpickers' strike led by the United Farm Workers in Yuma. Castro said this was the kind of thing you had to do to be a Chicano governor in "Goldwater country."

And Gov. Jerry Apodaca of New Mexico said even before he took office that he was not going to shake things up by appointing and hiring more Chicanos. In fact, he said he would be careful to avoid this.

These politicians, and any so-called communists who front for them, are not helping to fight the oppression of Chicanos. They are helping to maintain it by preaching faith in the political parties and the system responsible for that oppression.

Contrary to the CP's slanders, it is the serious Chicano nationalists who have been in the forefront of the struggle against bourgeois ideology in this country, through the formation of the Raza Unida parties independent of the capitalist-controlled Democratic and Republican parties. These parties point the way forward for the Chicano masses, who need to break from the capitalist parties and construct a mass party that would fight for the interests of Chicanos not only in the electoral arena, but in daily struggles as well.

The Raza Unida parties have also set an example for Blacks and for the labor movement as a whole, who would also benefit from forming a party of their own to fight the bosses' parties.

Far from being a middle-class ideology, Chicano nationalism has been the ideology of the most militant fighters against the capitalist class. It is to be found in the most oppressed layers of the Chicano community.

Contrary to the theories of the Communist party and the Maoist groups, the Chicano people are overwhelmingly working class in composition. A class of big capitalists does not even exist among Chicanos. The oppression of Chicanos as a people is tied in with the superexploitation of Chicanos as a discriminated-against section of the working class. Therefore, the aspiration of Chicanos for liberation as a people is a form of class consciousness. It is a limited form, just as trade-union consciousness is a limited form of class consciousness. But the role of socialists is not to condemn it, but to be in the forefront of all struggles for the rights of the Chicano people, while pointing to the connection of these struggles with the struggle of the working class as a whole.

Chicano culture

Those who claim to be socialists but oppose Chicano nationalism fail to see many issues that are of great importance to Chicanos. It is as if they had blinders on, and can see only the narrowest results of the oppression of Chicanos as wage earners.

They fail, for instance, to see the importance of demands for Chicano studies and the right to develop Chicano culture. These questions are especially important to an oppressed people. An integral part of the oppression of Chicanos is the destruction and suppression of the culture and true history of Chicanos. The capitalist rulers benefit from obliterating Chicano history because this keeps Chicanos from understanding how they came to be an oppressed people.

Those who think Chicano liberation can be achieved *simply* by adopting a culture different from that of Anglo society, without a political struggle, are obviously in a blind alley. But the struggle for the right to reclaim Chicano history, language, and culture is an important part of the effort of *la raza* to ascertain its true identity as an oppressed people. It can be a real factor in the struggle for national liberation. Therefore, Marxists look positively upon the development of Chicano arts, Chicano schools, and Chicano studies.

Leninism and Stalinism

The notion that nationalism of oppressed peoples is contradictory to the class struggle originates with the Stalinists—that is, with the followers of the Communist parties of Moscow and Peking, the heirs of Joseph Stalin. Their treacherous refusal to support national liberation struggles has nothing in common with the Marxist tradition, the tradition of Lenin, Trotsky, and the Russian Bolshevik party. Yet because the Stalinists claim to be Marxists and Leninists, they have succeeded in confusing millions of oppressed people throughout the world as to the true stand of Marxism in regard to national liberation.

The Stalinist bureaucracy that gained control in the Soviet Union made a mockery of the great ideals the Russian revolution stood for, not only in regard to the rights of oppressed nationalities, but in all areas of life. Workers' democracy, a cherished principle of the original revolutionary regime, was extinguished. Today there is no democracy in the Soviet Union. Anyone who voices disagreement with official policy is declared either counterrevolutionary or insane, and locked up. This has probably done more than anything else to discredit socialism in the eyes of workers throughout the world.

The Marxist position on national struggles of oppressed peoples was developed chiefly by Lenin, in the course of his experiences in the Russian revolution and in the leadership of the Communist International. His position was that revolutionary socialists must give full support to all oppressed peoples in the struggle against their oppressors. This includes the right to self-determination, even to the point of separation and forming their own state if that is what the oppressed people feel is necessary to assure their liberation.

The Bolshevik party was forced to deal with this question because it was a key aspect of the Russian revolution. Tsarist Russia was known as the "jailhouse of nations" because of the great number of oppressed nationalities forcibly retained within its borders. Only 43 percent of the population belonged to the dominant nationality, the Great Russians. The rest of the population—80 million people—was made up of oppressed peoples, including Ukrainians, Poles, Latvians, Estonians, and many others. Under the tsar, more than 650 laws existed that abridged the rights of Jews. Some peoples had formal equality under the law but were oppressed through enforced economic underdevelopment.

Clearly, in order to make a revolution it was necessary for revolutionists to address themselves to this oppression. It was necessary to win the confidence and support of the oppressed, most of whom in this case were not workers but peasants.

The reformist parties of Russia failed to champion the rights of the oppressed nationalities, often cloaking their indifference in rhetoric about internationalism. Lenin and the Bolsheviks, on the other hand, fought uncompromisingly for the right of these nations to secede from Russia if they so desired. For this, the reformists accused the Bolsheviks of wanting to "dismember" Russia.

But Lenin knew that a revolution could only succeed if the working class—which was made up largely of Great Russians—was able to win the support or at least acquiescence of the oppressed peoples. Separately, neither could win liberation. And, indeed, the oppressed peoples of Russia found that they had to turn to the working class and the fight for socialism—not the capitalist leaders—in order to win their national liberation.

Gravediggers with steam shovels
Despite many differences in the situations, the lessons of the Russian revolution on the national question are very perti-

nent to the United States today. Here, also, the development of capitalism has created oppressed nations within a nation, particularly in the case of Black people and Chicanos.

At the time of the Anglo conquest of the Southwest (or Northwest, depending on your point of view), a considerable number of the inhabitants of the northern part of Mexico were either small farmers or were living in semifeudal conditions. In Southern California, the *padres* (priests) established the hacienda-mission-presidio system and forced the Indians to work for them for no wages. The *indios* created through their labor a wealthy society with enormous herds of cattle and horses, and thriving agriculture. A racial caste system prevailed.

The U.S. invasion of 1848 destroyed all this. Over the years, the Mexican residents of the conquered territories, and the millions who came north later, were driven off the land and had to look for jobs in the cities.

But at the same time that capitalism was drawing Blacks and Chicanos into the working class, the ruling class maintained and deepened racist discrimination. That is, Blacks and Chicanos were not absorbed into the working class on an equal basis with Anglos. They were segregated and set apart in all areas of life as a sector of second-class citizens. They were forged into distinct peoples with a common history of oppression, common cultural heritage, common problems. In doing this, the capitalists have planted seeds of their own destruction.

As Marx taught, the dominant class under each form of class society gives rise to its own gravedigger—the oppressed classes. Capitalist society has created the working class. And in forging oppressed nationalities that are superexploited sections of the working class, you might say that U.S. capitalism has created a gravedigger with a steam shovel.

Black and Raza workers are not just the most oppressed sectors of the working class, they are also among the most powerful sectors. The Black population is approaching 25 million. The combined Chicano and Puerto Rican population is approaching 15 million. The total is nearly 40 million. Moreover, Black and Chicano workers are concentrated in the key sectors of the service and heavy industries. There are auto plants in Detroit and steel plants in Illinois and Indiana where Blacks are a majority of the work force. In Southern California Chicanos are a large percentage of the steelworkers. Growing numbers of Blacks and Chicanos are in key government and related jobs, such as in the postal system and public transportation. Among workers in these key services, the influence of the Chicano movement and the Black movement will be great.

As the most oppressed sector of the labor movement, Chicanos and Blacks will be the most militant fighters against the bosses and their government. They have the most to gain and nothing to lose.

The fact that they are the most militant fighters, together with their strategic position in the economy, indicates that Chicanos and Blacks are destined to be the vanguard of the American working class. They will be in the leadership of the American socialist revolution.

Combined revolution

Thus the coming American revolution will have to be a combined one, like the Russian revolution of 1917. It will be a combined process of winning equality and liberation for the oppressed nationalities, and a workers' revolution to do away with capitalist wage exploitation once and for all.

A revolutionary socialist program must address itself to this reality. It must combine demands and solutions that fight class as well as national oppression.

Those who want to separate out "workers' demands" from the social and political demands of the Chicano community can only begin from the unspoken assumption that the *real* working class is the Anglos. The Chicano worker is not only interested in wages, but also in the right of his or her children to bilingual-bicultural education, the right to equality in jobs and housing, the right not to be deported.

Moreover, the most crucial issues before the labor movement today are *not* simply wage demands, but questions such as the need to eliminate the war budget, defense of affirmative action plans, the fight for a shorter workweek at no cut in pay, the struggle over busing for desegregation, the need to forge unity between oppressed minorities and teachers and other government workers who are under attack, and independent political action by the entire labor movement.

The combined character of the struggle for socialism in this country also has implications for the kind of organization necessary to lead this struggle.

Some Chicanos who want to fight for Chicano liberation and socialism have formed Chicano socialist groups, collectives, or study circles. Some of these groups reject working together with other Chicanos who are not yet socialists in nationalist formations such as La Raza Unida party.

The spread of socialist ideas among Chicanos, as reflected in the rise of such groups, is very positive. But Chicano socialist groups are not sufficient to meet the needs of the struggle for Chicano liberation and socialism.

On the one hand, there is a need for an independent Chicano party that can involve all Chicanos who are ready to fight the racist policies of the Democrats and Republicans. Such a party can appeal to the masses of Chicanos at their present level of consciousness. At the same time it points in the direction of a break from the two capitalist parties by the working class as a whole. This is a step it must take if it is to challenge capitalist rule.

On the other hand, there is a need for a multinational revolutionary party, a party that brings together Anglo, Chicano, Black, and Puerto Rican revolutionists around a common program.

Multinational revolutionary party

As was cited earlier, the Leninist policy on the struggle for national liberation was crucial to the success of the Russian revolution. There was another side to the great contribution Lenin made on this subject, and that was on the need for a centralized revolutionary party uniting revolutionists of all nationalities within a country.

A party of the type Lenin developed is essential because of the centralized, ruthless character of our enemy, the capitalist class. In the face of this centralized opponent—with its police, FBI, courts, and other institutions for propaganda and repression—it is not sufficient to envision some kind of federation between Chicano socialists, Black socialists, and Anglo socialists.

A revolutionary party that hopes to take on the capitalists and win must be a totally different kind of organization. It must join revolutionists from both oppressor and oppressed nationalities on the basis of one revolutionary program. Through common experiences in the class struggle, these revolutionists can forge an organization that can act as one. Only such an organization will be capable of achieving unity in action by the entire working class to take the power and wealth out of the hands of the rich.

The Socialist Workers Party and the Young Socialist Alliance are building the nucleus of such a mass revolutionary party to lead the American socialist revolution. And we are in fraternal solidarity with the revolutionary socialists of the Fourth International in Mexico, Latin America, Europe, Africa, Asia, and the Middle East who are fighting for the same revolutionary program. Our program unites us with them, just as it unites revolutionists within the United States.

By joining in the struggle for socialism, Chicanos will not only be better able to further the liberation of their people; they will be making the greatest contribution possible to the liberation of all the oppressed peoples of the world from racism, capitalism, and imperialism.

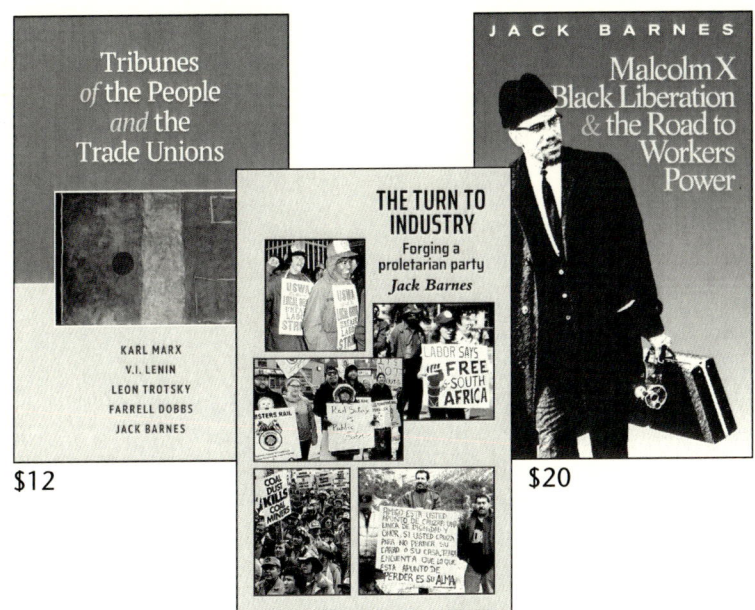

$12 $20

$15

Three books to be read as one . . .

about building a party that's working class in program, composition, and action. One that recognizes, in word and deed, the most revolutionary fact of our time . . .

. . . that working people have the power to create a different world as we act together to defend our own class interests—not those of the privileged classes who exploit our labor, not of those who fear us as "deplorables," or just plain "trash."

As we advance along a revolutionary course toward workers power, we will transform ourselves and awaken to our own worth. Also in Spanish, French, Farsi, Greek.

Special Offer!
All three $30

The Turn to Industry and *Tribunes of the People and the Trade Unions* $20

Either book plus *Malcolm X, Black Liberation, and the Road to Workers Power* $25

PATHFINDERPRESS.COM

CAPITALIST CRISIS AND THE FIGHT FOR WORKERS POWER

The Low Point of Labor Resistance Is Behind Us
The Socialist Workers Party Looks Forward

JACK BARNES
MARY-ALICE WATERS
STEVE CLARK

The global order imposed by Washington is shattering. A long retreat by the working class and unions has come to an end. The bosses and their government are stepping up attacks on our wages, conditions, and constitutional rights. This book highlights opportunities for building a mass proletarian party able to lead the struggle to end capitalist rule, opening a socialist future for humanity. $10. Also in Spanish, French, Greek.

FBI on Trial
The Victory in the Socialist Workers Party Suit Against Government Spying

MARGARET JAYKO

The record of a historic victory in the fight for political rights, including the 1986 federal court ruling against government spying and excerpts from trial testimony by SWP leaders Farrell Dobbs and Jack Barnes. $17

Are They Rich Because They're Smart?
Class, Privilege, and Learning Under Capitalism

JACK BARNES

Exposes growing class inequalities in the US and the self-serving rationalizations of well-paid professionals who think their "brilliance" equips them to "regulate" working people, who don't know what's in our own best interest. $10. Also in Spanish, French, Farsi, Arabic, Greek.

The Teamster Series
FARRELL DOBBS

Four books on the 1930s strikes, organizing drives, and political campaigns that transformed the Teamsters into a militant industrial union movement. Written by the organizer of these battles and leader of the Socialist Workers Party. A tool for workers seeking to use union power and advance the fight for a party of labor. $16 each, series $50. Also in Spanish. *Teamster Rebellion* is also available in French, Farsi, Greek.

The Clintons' Anti-Working-Class Record
Why Washington Fears Working People

JACK BARNES

What working people need to know about the profit-driven course of Democrats and Republicans alike over the last three decades. And the political awakening of workers seeking to understand and resist the capitalist rulers' assaults. $10. Also in Spanish, French, Farsi, Greek.

Opening Guns of World War III: Washington's Assault on Iraq
JACK BARNES

The murderous assault on Iraq in 1990–91 heralded increasingly sharp conflicts among imperialist powers, growing instability of capitalism, and more wars. Also includes:

1945: When US Troops Said 'No!'
by Mary-Alice Waters

Lessons from the Iran-Iraq War
by Samad Sharif

In *New International* no. 7. $14. Also in Spanish, French, Farsi.

PATHFINDERPRESS.COM

FURTHER READING

The Fight Against Jew-Hatred and Pogroms in the Imperialist Epoch
Stakes for the International Working Class

V.I. LENIN, LEON TROTSKY
FARRELL DOBBS, JAMES P. CANNON
JACK BARNES, DAVE PRINCE

Jew-hatred and pogroms—such as Hamas carried out on October 7, 2023—are part of the social convulsions and wars of the imperialist epoch. The authors explain why fighting Jew-hatred is decisive to the working class and oppressed nations of the world—and *what is to be done to end it*. $10. Also in Spanish, French, Greek.

New Expanded Edition!
Cosmetics, Fashion, and the Exploitation of Women
MARY-ALICE WATERS, JOSEPH HANSEN, EVELYN REED

"Norms of beauty and fashion are inseparable from the class struggle." That's the title of the opening chapter of this timely new edition of a lively 1950s debate in the *Militant*, a socialist newsweekly. How cosmetics and fashion monopolies rake in profits from social insecurities of women and adolescents. Why women's integration into the workforce and unions is a major advance in the fight for emancipation. A Marxist classic on the origins of women's oppression and the working-class road forward. $15. Also in Spanish, French, Farsi, Greek.

Our Politics Start with the World
JACK BARNES

The huge economic and cultural inequalities between imperialist and semicolonial countries, and among classes within them, are perpetuated by the workings of capitalism. To build parties able to lead the revolutionary struggle for power in our own countries, vanguard workers must be guided by a strategy to close this gap. In *New International* no. 13. $14. Also in Spanish, French, Farsi, Greek.

New!
Revolution and the Road to Peace in Colombia
The Example of the Cuban Revolution
FIDEL CASTRO

"No crime can be committed in the name of revolution," Fidel Castro declares, drawing from the example set by working people of Cuba as they took state power out of the hands of its capitalist rulers. In 2008, as part of efforts to end six decades of armed conflict in Colombia, he shared the exemplary record of Cuba's revolutionary struggle with the Revolutionary Armed Forces of Colombia (FARC) and the world. $10. Also in Spanish.

Cuba and the Coming American Revolution
JACK BARNES

This is a book about the example set by the Cuban people that socialist revolution is not only necessary—it can be made. A book about the struggles of workers and other exploited producers in the imperialist heartland, and the youth attracted to them. About the class struggle in the US, where the revolutionary capacities of working people are as utterly discounted by the ruling powers as were those of the Cuban toilers. $10. Also in Spanish, French, Farsi.

Labor, Nature, and the Evolution of Humanity
The Long View of History
FREDERICK ENGELS, KARL MARX
GEORGE NOVACK, MARY-ALICE WATERS

Without understanding that social labor, transforming nature, has driven humanity's evolution for millions of years, working people are unable to see beyond the capitalist epoch of class exploitation that warps all human relations, ideas, and values. $12. Also in Spanish and French.

PATHFINDERPRESS.COM

PATHFINDER AROUND THE WORLD

UNITED STATES
(and Caribbean, Latin America, and East Asia)
> Pathfinder Books, 306 W. 37th St., 13th Floor
> New York, NY 10018

CANADA
> Pathfinder Books, 7107 St. Denis, Suite 204
> Montreal, QC H2S 2S5

UNITED KINGDOM
(and Europe, Africa, Middle East, and South Asia)
> Pathfinder Books, 5 Norman Rd.
> Seven Sisters, London N15 4ND

AUSTRALIA
(and New Zealand, Southeast Asia, and the Pacific)
> Pathfinder Books, Suite 2, First floor, 275 George St.
> Liverpool, Sydney, NSW 2170
> Postal address: P.O. Box 73, Campsie, NSW 2194

BUILD YOUR LIBRARY!
JOIN THE PATHFINDER READERS CLUB

$10 / YEAR
25% DISCOUNT ON ALL PATHFINDER TITLES
30% OFF BOOKS OF THE MONTH
Valid at pathfinderpress.com and local Pathfinder book centers

Go to: pathfinderpress.com/
products/pathfinder-readers-club

Pathfinder
pathfinderpress.com